Wreath of Desire

DOROTHEA BISBAS

i

Library of Congress Control Number: 2002096295

ISBN#: 978-0-9726423-0-9

Printed in the United States by:
Morris Publishing
3212 East Highway 30
Kearney, NE 68847
1-800-650-7888

This book of poetry is divided by a life-line; where my Grandmother's journey ends and mine begins.

She taught me courage. She showed me vision. She gave me love. I leave these gifts for her great grandchildren's children, with the hope that all that she was runs now in their veins.

For Cameron, Christiana, Morgan, Spencer, Alexa, Nicole, Ryan, Mason, and Devon. She loves you all through me.

The cover for this book was designed from a photograph taken in Greece by Duane Paul Munk, who encouraged me to write these poems and many more.

The formatting and photo-ready type-setting was prepared in friendship by Jan Hasman, always supportive in my efforts.

My Thursday poetry group has been my inspiration.

With Thanks,

Dorothea Bisbas

CONTENTS

❧

THE STORYTELLER

I was three or four,
still sucking my thumb, that age.
She would take me on her lap,
that warm, voluminous space, where
her apron scrunched when I sat
and soap and talc surrounded her fresh,
like the smell of snow forming in the air.

Her skin was bland against the black
she always wore, for her first-born,
buried young,
her hair braided tight in a coil at the back
of a neck that had bent over sadness
more than once,
the bun imprisoned with long hairpins
shaped more like mountain roads
than the other way around.

My thumb and finger would caress her ear,
a large lobe with a long thin line
where the pierced earring
had stretched it,
useless gold coins from the old country,
where the pain came from.

She'd begin in Greek.
We only spoke that ancient tongue, she and I,
as if it were a secret that we shared.
"Once in the old times" she'd always say.
Long tales, half truths, half myths,
of goat herders playing flutes and men
who flew wax-winged in the sun
and girls who danced on grapes.

Outside, a million tiny drummers beat
the rain gutters and lightning
sliced the sky in half, but I was safe
in that cave where nothing could reach me
but the folds of a grandmothers love.

≈

At night she'd free her hair.
It fell in sterling
rivers on her flannel robe
and she looked younger then and soft.
Stroking with her tattered brush
she'd hum a tune -
I've heard that song
a hundred different ways since then,
winding out of a licorice clarinet that
wailed like a lost child in the night,
plinked on a family mandolin or a bouzouki,
wild as a lusting lover,
the players feet tapping time.
Keeping time.
Keeping time.
Or on some 45 rpm
the voices high and whining,
the pain the same,
always the same pain
"Samiotisa, Samiotisa, poti tha pas sti Samo?"
Greek island girl of Samos, when
will you come home?

Betrothed at seventeen.
The family of the groom collected gifts
the dowry agreed upon was thirty drachmas
and a new born lamb,
the going price for love
a fair amount for the blue eyed man
twice her age.

Veiled in tulle too sheer to
hide her shyness, a white shroud,
she saw him for the first time at the altar.
They walked around a table
Isaiah's' dance in a ring,
the candles blurring
the circle of her captivity.

Tradition was her jailer,
ignorant and old, wearing
a priests embellished robe and chanting
Byzantine mysteries.

That night
they slept together in the same room
with his parents and siblings and
the thousand eyes of night -
poverty knows no privacy
then or now.
The sounds of lust roared
in her crimson shame,
she swallowed salt that slid
into her mouth,
her innocence in a heap
with his discarded clothes
in a room too dark for shadows but
a flimsy cover that would not,
for all her prayer
blanket her humiliation
or turn,
please God, turn
into day.

But morning mortified her too.
They raised the blood stained sheet
high on a pole and carried it to town
proof that she had married pure.

≈

When the dome of her belly began
to make uneven hems of her skirt,
they went to their own place to live
meager, dirt floored but apart,
with one window to the Meteora
the awesome rocks
where the monastery perched like an eagle
its cloudless aerie
a thousand feet in the sky
and one window to the olive trees,
rooted in the earth like wisdom
with their dusty silver leaves
and fields of tired vines
too old to bear their purple fruit
their wombs dry from giving
clinging to the earth from memory only.
Here,
she waited.

Soon a trail of flattened weeds disclosed
her daily pilgrimage
to the side of the rocks where
holy men secluded themselves
from humanness.
Standing in the shade of that pious place
she prayed
to a god in whose power
she was certain.

≈

As the baby in her grew
she sang to it
a mixed up lullaby and prayer
    be whole
    be beautiful
    be male

A girl was born to her
alone, in the fields
where she hoed.
She cried for help and
no one heard
except the blackbirds
flying close enough to mock.
The cries from the child mocked them back.
Now they were two
mother and daughter
their fates sealed in blood
spilled on the rocky soil
while gods in Olympus sent
Hermes to welcome them
to the secret world of pain
known only to women.

                                         ৡ

In time, another girl was born,
the temblor of birth tended by an old
and trusted midwife, strong enough to wall
the father out
soft enough to fill the room
corner to corner with
the bond of femininity
like a gentle light.

They named her Eva for the first woman.
She was a cameo of her mother,

as if, looking in a distant mirror
a small refracted image waited there.

Sophia hugged her sister like a doll
cooing the same sounds of love
she had learned
when she herself was suckling.

At night, she'd watch him watching them,
his amber beads, the komboloi,
flicking in his hands.
His worry beads, his balm.
The oil of the holy lamp burned beneath the icon
making long dark smudges on
the whitewashed wall.

Once he even told her that he loved her
the way he loved the warmth
of a summer month.

It was midnight
when he held the candle to her face
as she lay on their quilts,
milk still dribbling from the mouth of the babe
snuggled to her breast.

Some summer smells filled the air
dust and wild grasses and the starch
of his just laundered shirts, even
the voluptuous scent of her body's sweat
and the sour wine of his breath.

He startled her awake,
his shadow on the wall frightening her
the elongated blackness of him
the dark side
the one she was afraid to know.

He gathered some belongings in an old
valise that was peeling where
the weather had eroded the paisley print
some shirts and pants and socks
the ordinary only.
I will write when I can, he said,
telling her he was fleeing from the law.
Telegraph monies had been lost
where he worked.
He swore his innocence and disappeared
along with the shadow on the wall,
without even holding her for a minute
or kissing his daughters goodbye.

And the tears she felt rushing
were not for him
not for his leaving
not for any reason but her fear
that when a letter came
she could never read it.
She had never learned how.

࿘

She began the life of a widow,
though he had not died,
her grief taking on the shapelessness
of mourning, from absolute abandonment
to shame or fear
and the ultimate strength of anger.

The village spoke in clattered tongues
hurling verbal stones through
the already shattered windows of her life.
She learned to stand even taller, blameless
carrying her baby on her hip
her older daughter clinging to her skirts
when she walked to the well and back
never looking left or right
where the black-garbed gossipers sneered.

She raised the water in a pail,
the metal bands surrounding like a girdle
that kept the wood from splitting
from the swell
and when she bent to pour into her jug
she saw her fractured image there
her only friend.

Sometimes her mother came
shaking her head, cursing the fates
"Ach, ach, vlastima tin mira sou"
bringing hot, aromatic bread
upon which she had baked a cross of dough
to protect this family of women
and to keep the evil spirits away
she muttered obscure prayers over them
and hung odiferous strings of garlic
around their necks.

When her mother had clucked down the road
she took the garlic and hung it on the rafters
next to the basil drying
perfuming the air with its sweetness
next to the strong oregano
and the spearmint that grew wild and green
which she twisted into garlands
for Sophia's hair.
Then she folded her children to her
as if they needed nothing but each other.

There was no money now
and no place to face except the sun
which rose and set indifferently
as it always had
reminding her tomorrow would always be there
ready or not ready
with unbearable sameness.

She grew their food herself
close to the house, in nature's music,
wind hissing in the wheat,
birds so familiar their songs were words
and her own spirit singing a rhythmic chant
while she tuned the soil with a primal beat
to receive and return with its ancient wisdom.

อ

One day a letter came.
It was a village event -
everyone knew before she did
the letter was from America.
The postman tipping his hat ever so slightly
as she tucked the letter in her apron pocket
and disappeared into her house.

Four days went by before her pride
sitting in her mouth like raw vinegar
could be swallowed enough to take the letter
to someone who could read.

Rosemary tucked in her hair
gave her an air of confidence,
the jauntiness of the spring,
the perfect illusion
to present herself to her husbands brother
to have the message read.

He was fingering some amber beads,
a stream of smoke slithered from
the side of his mouth,
the bubble of the hookah
filling the air with a drugging mustiness
as he filtered Turkish tobacco
into his addiction.

She stood as he read
her back straight as a candle
never allowing her face to show
how frightened she really was
her stomach feeling as if a cat were clawing it.

Three tickets would arrive, she heard,
for passage to America
America
the word threaded itself slowly
through the eye of her memory

there, she had been told,
milk and honey were forever on the tongue
and the streets were rivers of gold.

Her mind rode the wings of hearsay
and pictured something new for herself
somewhere away from here.

꙳

She had never left the village.
She knew only the donkey trails
to the well and back
to the baker and back
to the church and back
and only in her mind had she
ever seen the sea
or the life in a city or
the gathering of great numbers of people.

On the way home she thought long thoughts
about what kept a ship afloat in the water
about never seeing her mother again
about life with a man
she no longer remembered
except in some forgotten dream.
But something sheer and fluttering
came over her lightly
like the touch of a moth -
a glimpse of hope.

The next day was Sunday.
She took communion at the church
and all the eyes upon her
felt like cold hard rain,
the Kyrie Eleison clanging in her head
like the gong that bid them all to kneel.
Lord have mercy, Lord have mercy
she said the words aloud for her own
heart to hear
Kyri Eleison, Kyri Eleison
Lord have mercy.

ॐ

It was decided that Sophia would stay behind.
Americans frowned on imperfections
and the child had a limp
from a bone that healed poorly
where the mule had kicked her
it would be best to send her later
with her Mother and Father already there
so the newsmonger said

and that is how she took her youngest child
and her husband's brother
the one avoiding the military
and began the journey into her destiny.

Eva turned seven
the year of the journey
she had her first ride on a donkey
side saddle with her mother
her uncle mounting the lead
short and pompous
as the villagers shouted their messages
now it was "sto kalo, Theos mazi sas"
go in peace, God be with you
where were those wishes in the long years
the hungry times
the lonely times
the endless times.

The donkeys plodded on
indifferent to everything
even the feel of the rocks on their hooves.
Sophia, left behind, held
her grandmother's hand, her world
shrinking into people growing smaller.

The sky darkened
the color of a moth
wrenching away the safety of the light

swallowing the sun and all who traveled west.
The Meteora loomed large
covering the village in grotesque images
and Sophia in grief.

By the time they reached the train,
my grandmother told me,
she could no longer remember
her daughter's face
so desperate was her need to see it
and all the pictures in her mind were headless
like a nightmare she could not erase.

Eva was enchanted with the velvet
seats and the scenery spinning by
and the man who punched a hole in her ticket
and pinched her cheek
"Is this Papa?" she asked.
They ate some bread and cheese and
greasy olives that stained their fingers brown,
Calamatas, from the trees
that grew beside the door
that she had left behind
with everything else she had ever known.

≈

When they arrived in Athens
she was a thousand years older
she felt that she was hanging in time
not knowing the way forward or back.

There at last was the ocean
for as far as she could see
the horizon met the water
merging like lovers
and even the bustling wharf

with its briny smells and raucous sounds
could not detain her eye
so had the sea captivated her.

They were herded into steerage
crowded and cheerless
with frightened eyes peering
from fringed shawl covered faces and
children clinging to floor sweeping skirts.

Men and women separated into spaces
like the goats they themselves
had prodded into pens.
Gentle goat herders, so many of them
from the hills
and the voyage began
one day, one day after the other
each day like the one before
until the news came to them
that they were being quarantined.

They were taken to an island
somewhere off the coast of Italy
where each day the launch
took them to a small beach
to lie in the sun until the ban,
like a black banner over their heads,
could be lifted.

They walked in the sand and
gathered in groups to sing
the old songs.
They all knew them by the heart
that had lived in them since birth
along with the blood that ran in their veins.
Sad songs about love and war

and about the soil
they might never see again

    the Greek soil
    the blessed soil
    they cried with the memory.

And after two long weeks of this
this limbo
they were on their way again
to the new kind of heaven.

❧

There was no way they could have known
the malice of the sea
that took their ship and tossed it
side to side
trying to rid the waves of their burden

and they lay hour after hour
the pit of their stomachs in their mouths
trying to reach the next hour
    the next minute
    the next second
until they relinquished their lives to the fates
and slept in fitful spurts
one eye open to fear
and the other wishing for death
so that a death easier than living
became their dreams.

Clustered together
with the intuition of wild olive trees
they knew they would arrive
    beyond the revenge of the sea
    beyond the threat of dying
    beyond the terror of tomorrow

and when the long awaited lady
came into view
they cried with terrified joy.

It was night and her torch
cast the first warmth on the waters
like a smile on the face
of the mothers they tried to remember
from the other side of themselves.

&

They waited on deck all night
like nervous bridegrooms
to step in that cathedral of hope
that island
where white robed gods waited to decide
who were the strong.
And the weak shuddered
at their own flaws and hurried
to hide them in the new world clothes
they had been saving for this day.

She left her feather bedding
and some bulging baggage
at the entrance, with a prayer
for its safety
and carried the silver icon with her,
the one of the Virgin and Jesus
that she could not bear to
leave among strangers.

Their manifests took them to the great
registry to be reckoned
one by one
like the judgment day.

Iron rails steered them to their fate,
cryptic letters chalked their coats
H, K, X and the dreaded E for eyes
that would send the bearer back
faulty human freight.

She kept her gaze on the flag
her heart pounding, fearful,
but when they questioned her
she answered firmly
and when they asked if she could read
she simply shook her head.

She clutched the papers with the seal of entry
as if she had been given the key to life
and was herded beyond the great Hall
where the waiting faces peered
to meet the weary and the anxious
who had come past the Island of Tears.

≈

He stood apart, blond, his eyes
the color of the Aegean Sea
and she remembered him, barely,
as if seeing him through her sheer
wedding veil.

Shyness rose to her face
and left a stamp of color there,
her mind corroded with misgivings
served her poorly now
but the specter from the past,
the apparition of a caustic man,
fell like a withered leaf
when she saw his shattered face

his body bent
a look of pain even in the clothes he wore.

In those final steps
she saw the armband on his sleeve.
Black, the blackest
black for mourning
he took her hands and said it was Sophia,

Sophia who had died
from something they could not explain
while her mother crossed the waters.
He had learned of it by wire
the morning of that very day.

≈

There was never any joy now
just sleeping and waking
and the time between a fitful torture
as she dragged her black garbed body
from day to dreaded day
wishing herself dead.

Eva was so young
the harness of her innocence
kept her loving life.
She laughed and played as ever
so far was her sisters face
from this new adventure.

"Take off that dress, Mama"
she'd say of the somber black
"and come play with me"
but she never did
till more and more, this child
excluded by the wall of mourning
became morose

and sick with lack of love
until she lay in bed lifeless like her parents
and the eclipse was total.

And then,
my grandmother told me,
the child's sad face shook her from her sorrow.
She lifted her only daughter and held her high
to the God she thought had betrayed her
and promised

if her health returned
she would give her all the love
that she had buried with the other girl.

So when Eva came to life again
they took the armbands from their sleeves
and burned them in the fire
of the wood burning stove
their guilt curling into ash

and then they joined hands and danced
round and round the kitchen table
holding their hands high and singing
loving the touch of each other.

And the years came and went
in predictable procession, except for the baby
she could never seem to conceive
and the sadness that came every month
until she folded that hope away too
with the other linens of her mind
that could never be worn.

≈

She would learn some foreign ways
the names of streets that felt thick
to her tongue
some numbers
and a new style of dressing,
stylish, but severe and ever black.

But every patch of blue
was the Greek sky
every child in the park
was Sophia
every kindly face
was her mother's.

Next to her icons she kept
a small silk pouch full of earth
from the old country
it was holy.

She began to work
in a sweat shop with other women.
The hum of the machines a chorus of zithers.
She spoke no English
so Eva ran around the shop
turning the unfamiliar words into Greek
or Armenian
or Polish
so natural was it for the child
so difficult for the others.

They heated their lunch,
meat and bread,
on the tops of radiators.
An aroma hung in the air
like the magic from a dozen kitchens
and they wove bits of gossip into the day
as if they were the threads of silk
from the chemises they were sewing.

≈

At twenty four, Eva married
a man of spiritual sense and magnanimity
and took her parents to her home,
so bonded had they become
and they lived in her life now
as the girth of love grew
to nurture two children
one of which was me.

I was raised in the smile of her voice
singing the old songs
telling the old tales

and by her gentle hands
that kneaded sweet anise bread
in my mothers kitchen,
her back straight as the spindle of her bedpost,
her eyes brown as the rich earth
filling with tears, sometimes,
at the words she sang,
"Samiotisa, Samiotisa, poti tha sto Samo?"

Greek island girl of Samos
when will you come home?

≈

Prologue To A Greek Journey

I hear your voices
you are the mothers of my mother
calling me home
the hum of history
twists through my veins
as rooted as your vines

I will come to you on a peeling boat
its lantern a moon on the water
I will sail to your alabaster shore
show me your conical trees
your purple grapes, red poppies
blowing kisses to the rocks
your ancient stones piled in temples
the white washed houses of your children
the villages that never change
I will walk your winding roads
with a gnarled stick carved with myths
to lead me to that place
where I was begun

I will gather nuts and melons on the way
light candles at your wayside altar
stand in the shadow of myself
and feel my blood

KALAMBAKA , AT THE METEORA

She sits at the threshold of darkness
the room behind her steeped and shadowed
with early evening.
She pulls a cotton thread through her fingers
tatting as if by rote, an intricate memory
she assigns to her hands, hands with the memory
of a spider spinning.
She speaks to me as I stand
in her willful garden
hyacinths and poppies playing
against the breeze.

Pethaki mou, my child, who are you?
I step outside myself to find the answer.
How can I answer without conviction?
I am still on that endless journey
to find that very thing.
I am a child of this village, I tell her.
My grandmother was born here
I am here to walk in her life.
From her pocket she pulls a strand of beads
amber in color with a marble eye at the end.
She says it will keep evil spirits away.

I search my purse for something,
something to exchange for this protection.
Among the Hollywood contents I find
a scarf, blue, a color she has long ago
deserted for the yoke of black.

She runs it through her hands
feeling the silk, the clouded
membrane of her eyes straining to see.
Around my neck I hang the glaring eye

If evil spirits are here
they will look away
leaving me to search alone.
They will know there is nothing
in this land I do not love.

Tomorrow
I begin my ascent to the monasteries,
the Meteora,
those aeries on monoliths in the sky.
The soul of my grandmother leads the way.

෨

Meeting Yesterday

I expected the cobalt dome
that intense jewel blue of the sky
I expected those rotund cupolas
their crosses jutting in the air
the blue and whiteness of it all
the transparent sea
montages of thalo under aquamarine

I didn't know about the stones

not the stones piled high in temples
that honor omnipotent gods
or even the Parthenon
that adamant tribute shrouded in decay

under my feet
mixed with tiny weeds and gritty soil
the crushed rubble of time

those stones

I put one to my lips
my tongue touches the chalky angles
I taste the salt of wars
the warmth of the Aegean sun
the endurance of this place
the soul of the ancients
the genesis of wisdom
the dust of progress

I carry this stone everywhere
its weight
a nudging reminder of
why I am here

WREATH OF DESIRE

This Sunday, silence cools the air.
Nearby the scent of incense
smokes through the church doors
where all the villagers have gone to pray.

Alone here at a doorway,
its blue paint flaking beneath
a wreath of lilacs
dried from another season.
A tiny key clings to a rusty nail.

I covet that key
want to enter the door
throw open the dusty shutters
wave a lacy handkerchief
at all the passersby
calling them by name
as if I'd always lived there

as if that bed with its tattered quilt
that spindly chair
those tintographs on the flowered wall
were mine
and I had been born in that room
I want to live that life,
that Greek life,
for a little while.

Mountain in Thessaly

Work of ages, Pelion
cloistered here in cypress shade
like pottery shards from some forgotten time.
Your roads are pine banked
slick with rain weaving high
above the lights of distant towns
whose air is jealous of the headiness of yours.

Place of peace, Pelion.
the sound of quiet swaddles like the womb
only the breath of chestnut trees is heard
and sometimes a horse neighing
or a tiny dog barking
to reassure himself
there is such a thing as noise.

the smell of soil is rich
like coffee brewing
dark, promising comfort.

Deer nibble at lush ground
as if it were a lovers breast
gently, but with purpose.

I sleep that night on the forest floor
to feel my history beneath me.

PORTRAIT OF AN HOUR IN KIFISIA

In the tiny cove
turquoise waves spank the rocks
as if they'd misbehaved
the only other sound a bleating goat
led by a barefoot girl

she picks a shell from the beach
turning it over and over
as if the secret of life
lies in its hollow hull

above on cliffs
the old men tip their chairs
to the sun
in some ancient rite
they gather to sip the black coffee
sweetened with self importance

at the bakers oven
the women come and go
dependable like the waves
their warm anise bread
scentilates the air

now a donkey bray is carried on the wind
like some primal pain
two small boys prod him on
kicking stones as they go

I watch a woman standing in her window
lace curtains billow around her
like a wedding gown
does she wonder where her love will come from?

An Open Door

Here among the myrtle grove
where sea salts the air
where fishermen mend their nets
and bougainvillea splashes the white-washed houses
where women hide their hair in black mystery
I find a church with an open door

From my terror haunted world
where fear
paralyzes welcome
a touch of madness in the eye
of every stranger
what buoyant comfort to find
an open door

I enter and feel a hallowed moment
the visible expressing the invisible
Byzantine collections of old beliefs
censed with smoky myrrh
and the flickering glances of tapers
the splendor of old polished wood

I kneel at the white draped altar
a candle warm in my hands
remembering all those whose blood
runs through my veins
remembering I am the last to remember them
praying to keep my heart
an open door

GRAVEYARD IN MACEDONIA

North of the Vale of Tempe
in the shadow of Olympus
a tiny village, older than the inner eye
preserves its ancestry

we visit the graveside there
at Kokinoplo
where a collection of bones
the color of eggshells
are piled like discarded shoes
in cardboard boxes
in a room smaller than a closet

unearthed femurs and cracked ulnas
phalanges picked clean by time
wait
all grotesquely wait
for the claiming of the quick

a bearded monk palms a skull
"this is your grandfather," he says
behind him hot winds snake through the wild wheat
hissing
blowing his black robes around him
fanning a scent of incense and candle wax and sweat

the Greek sky domes like a jewel case for clouds
that settle on the mountain in pearl clusters

only the cypress and the daphne remember
how long the breezes have come and gone
blowing dust into that open room

where it clings like a friendly cat
waiting to be brushed aside

the boxes fill every space
there is no room now
for even the smallest bones

&

PASTORALE

she gathers wood
each piece a child she
swaddles in her burlap sack
slung close to the breasts
dried decades past

she will bake bread
for her toothless man
who will eat the soft center
like lust
sharing another hour
they live past the cocks crow
again

tomorrow they will
like the bread she bakes
rise
a prayer close to breath forming
on their open mouths
silence is the bramble of their years

cars will glisten by
slick and swift
centuries ahead
here in their humble space
the only feeling they still fuel is
being

Woman of Metsovo

I see her coming from the bakers oven
a huge round tray balanced on her head
aromas of goat cheese and spinach
that tradition in papery crust
we smile

What is that moment between strangers
that transcends shyness and fear
that awakens a familiarity
even a bond
allowing the moment to create a memory
as if a photo is snapped
as if we see with our hearts

She stops to talk, all the while
her steaming cargo settled on her turban
I must seem as rare to her
my denim jeans my western shirt
a global contrast to her embroidered skirt
her sturdy black shoes

she asks if I would visit her and I go
following close to that pan of food
that sends me tumbling to that inner place
where food and love are the same

in her home we drink water
colored red with cherries
that settle to the bottom of the glass
we scoop them up with a long handled spoon
savoring the syrupy dregs

we speak of this place
this mountain air dense with daphne and pine
the cobbled streets from a century forgotten
the tapestries that fill the village stores

when we say goodbye there is a sadness in her eyes
the kind a mother feels seeing her child grow too fast
in mine is a startling wonder
that things can be so invincible

streets of stone
food that awakens the spirit
woman meeting woman

࿔

ADMONITIONS TO THE GODS

Almond trees are blooming in Delphi
where Homer sang
where laurels wreathed the idols
Apollo and his priests

I must tell you now in Delphi
where many stood laced in fear
to hear your thunder
the locusts have eaten your words
your oracles are done

Dethroned by men of genius
the poet Pindar
gifted hands of Phidias
platinum tongue of Plato
Socrates the thinker

I am their daughter
marrow of their bones
and I have come to claim my power
earth of light
sky of wisdom
brilliant sea
they are mine

a gift from my mothers

AGIOS YIANNIS

Time has folded its wings here
this tiny town we stumble on
at the bottom of an untamed mountain
the sea stretches like a blue whale
rising in graceful swells
sleek and lithe
nuzzling the sun bleached rocks that hug the shore

forget all the Byzantine splendors
the temples built to Zeus, Athena,
the palace of Knossos,
the Parthenon, acropoli,
museum jars of broken shards
here is Greece
being only what it is
and nothing more

We swim in the tepid water
without our clothes, our past
our future
We dine in taverns on the beach
Fish, their wide eyes clinging to their last moment.
Bread, warm as comfort,
cheese, salty as the gulf
and smooth onyx colored olives
we sleep an afternoon sleep
sun-worn, senses pleasured
we sleep a heavy sleep

We wake to read, to drink
the cloudy ouzo
in geranium air, on a shuttered balcony
far from the packed suitcase of my mind
in the sweet, inaudible hum
of timelessness at Agios Yiannis

St. Stephans in the Sky

Past the thickness of old oak doors
past the skulls displayed like trophies
on wooden shelves,
of monks who had lived and died here
extraordinary, ordinary men,
past the discernment of nuns
eying our savvy clothes
our permed hair
our shadowed eyes,
nuns who drape us in ragged skirts
to cover our naked legs,
we enter the sanctity of
the monastery chapel.

Holy place, where seclusion
was harmless and neutral
how did the war find you?
The Nazi bayonets plunged deep
into your sacred icons,
Mary and Jesus riddled with bullets
their eyes void of judgment.

I stand before you ashamed
that nothing has changed
and war is still a constant
and respect is still a distant drum.

MIDNIGHT MOVES

We wait for the pulse to throb
late parties in the taverns by the sea
serving food mostly about salt
tiny rings of calamari
olives black and shiny
as the eyes of Greek women
eggplant smothered in garlic
snow white cubes of goats' milk

Ouzo on ice brings euphoria
sip after cloudy sip
now the music starts
a wild eyed bouzouki player
strumming his heart strings
a clarinetist wailing licorice notes
that wind in the smoky air
guitars amplify our heartbeats
as we tap our feet
to the pain and love

Three men circle their shoulders
their feet finding precision so perfect
they are one body
we join them
a circle of shoes tipping to the music

Someone throws a plate

it cracks into a hundred chips

we dance around the wasteful tribute
celebrating being alive
being joyfully exuberant
being Greek

Zimbayako

Come, I will dance with you
the wild, willful dance of lust
you dare not dance without me

raise your hands to the sun, close your eyes
the thunder of your heart will guide your steps
slow, slow at first, then faster
faster
do not let old womens tongues
bind your feet

smell the salt sting the Aegean air
taste the breeze, warm
with the clarity of ouzo
hold this cigarette
let the smoke cloud your eyes with vision
see life as you want it to be

slow, slow at first, then faster
faster
let joy swell your breast
till your nipples bristle
with passion
kiss this soil where we dance
the bones of Socrates bleached white
are graveled here
the sun has coaxed the cypress and the olive
to dress your naked eye

lift your skirts to Olympus
the whiteness of your thighs
will dazzle the gods
make love in your dance
slow, slow at first, then faster, faster
they who do not dance will think us mad